Big Machines That Build

by Brienna Rossiter

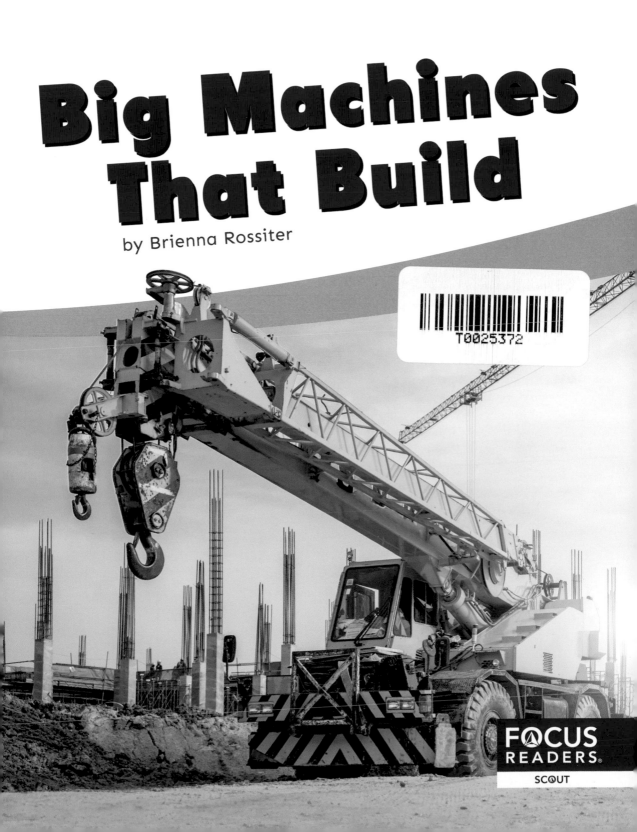

FOCUS
READERS.

SCOUT

www.focusreaders.com

Focus Readers is distributed by North Star Editions:
sales@northstareditions.com | 888-417-0195

Produced for Focus Readers by Red Line Editorial.

Photographs ©: Shutterstock Images, cover, 1, 4 (top), 4 (bottom), 7 (top), 7 (bottom), 9, 11 (top), 11 (bottom), 13, 15, 16 (top left), 16 (bottom left), 16 (top right), 16 (bottom right)

Library of Congress Cataloging-in-Publication Data
Names: Rossiter, Brienna, author.
Title: Big machines that build / Brienna Rossiter.
Description: Lake Elmo, MN: Focus Readers, 2021. | Series: Big machines |
   Includes index. | Audience: Grades K-1
Identifiers: LCCN 2020036696 (print) | LCCN 2020036697 (ebook) | ISBN
   9781644936764 (hardcover) | ISBN 9781644937129 (paperback) | ISBN
   9781644937846 (pdf) | ISBN 9781644937488 (ebook)
Subjects: LCSH: Construction equipment--Juvenile literature. | Cranes,
   derricks, etc.--Juvenile literature. | Earthmoving machinery--Juvenile
   literature.
Classification: LCC TH900 .R6326 2021 (print) | LCC TH900 (ebook) | DDC
   624.028/4--dc23
LC record available at https://lccn.loc.gov/2020036696
LC ebook record available at https://lccn.loc.gov/2020036697

Printed in the United States of America
Mankato, MN
012021

About the Author

Brienna Rossiter is a writer and editor who lives in Minnesota. She loves being outside and having campfires.

Trucks 5

Cranes 8

More Machines 10

Glossary 16

Index 16

Trucks

A dump truck holds a **load**.

The truck has a bed.

The bed tips up.

This truck mixes **concrete**.

It has a drum.

The drum spins.

Concrete comes down a **chute**.

drum

chute

Cranes

A crane lifts loads.

It has a hook.

It lifts big and heavy things.

More Machines

A paver makes roads.

It lays **asphalt**.

A road roller makes it flat.

A bulldozer moves dirt.

It rolls on tracks.

It pushes the dirt.

track

This machine digs holes.

It has a bucket.

It scoops up dirt.

bucket

Glossary

asphalt

concrete

chute

load

Index

B
bulldozer, 12

D
dump truck, 5

P
paver, 10

R
road roller, 10